# THE
## LITTLE _of_ BOOK
# CHRISTMAS

Christmas time! That man must be a misanthrope indeed, in whose breast something like jovial feeling is not roused, in whose mind some pleasant associations are not awakened, by the recurrence of Christmas . . . A Christmas family party! We know of nothing in nature more delightful! There seems a magic in the very name of Christmas.

Charles Dickens *Sketches by Boz* (1836)

# CONTENTS

# NATIVITY AND THE CHRISTMAS CRIB

*In 1224, St. Francis of Assissi asked the Pope's permission
to celebrate Christmas by recreating the nativity scene,
complete with live ox and ass, at Grecchio. Cribs had existed
in Rome since at least 649, but it was St. Francis's depiction
that captured the medieval imagination and established the
cult of the crib throughout Christian Europe.*

*Thereafter, cribs not only became a feature in churches at
Christmas time, they also became household objects.
Intricately carved models, cribs with musical boxes and even
clockwork cribs were produced in Austria, Bavaria and even
Protestant Germany. Cribs continued to be popular in France,
Spain and Italy but were not imported to England and the
United States until the middle of the 19th century. Even then,
cribs were not common outside Roman Catholic churches,
presumably because of their Popish origins, until
well into this century.*

# THE LITTLE BOOK of CHRISTMAS

*by*
*JENNIFER MULHERIN*

**Crescent Books**

This 1991 edition published by Crescent Books,
distributed by Outlet Book Company Inc.,
a Random House Company, 225 Park Avenue South,
New York, New York 10003

ISBN 0-517-06537-1

*CREDITS*
Editor: *Catriona Luce*
Designer and color artwork: *Pauline Bayne*
Typesetting: *SX Composing Ltd.*
Color separation: *Chroma Graphics (Overseas) Pte. Ltd.*
Printed in Belgium
8 7 6 5 4 3 2 1

# CHRISTMAS DAY

*SURPRISINGLY, THERE IS LITTLE EVIDENCE TO SUGGEST THAT Christ was born on 25 December. Indeed, Christmas Day did not officially come into being until 354 when Pope Gregory proclaimed 25 December as the date of the Nativity. In doing this, he was following the Church's policy of absorbing rather than repressing ancient pagan rites, for the winter solstice and the coming of spring had been celebrated since early times.*

*The pagan festival most closely associated with the new Christmas was the Roman Saturnalia, which honoured the god Saturn on 17 December and was followed by several days of feasting, revelry and anarchy, when masters waited on slaves and servants, wantoness was condoned and civil disorder was ignored.*

*In 1552, the English Puritans banned Christmas, a move followed in Massachussetts seven years later. Although Christmas returned to England with Charles II in 1660, the rituals all but lapsed until revived in tamer form in Victorian times.*

# THE TWELVE DAYS
# OF CHRISTMAS

THE TWELVE DAYS OF CHRISTMAS, ALTHOUGH NOW LARGELY
*associated with Christian rituals, date back to the pagan
Yuletide feast of northern Europe. This was held at the time of
the winter solstice and lasted 12 days. The origins of Yuletide
itself lay in prehistoric days when, to encourage the dying sun
to new life, primitive peoples lit bonfires to give the sun
light and warmth.*

*No one knows when Yule logs were first ceremoniously carried
into Norsemen's dwellings, but from the Middle Ages the
custom was well established in northern Europe. A huge log,
chosen from a forest tree, was dragged home and decorated
with greenery and ribbons. After it was dried, it was burned
over the 12 days of Yuletide: Nordic people believed that this
had a magical effect in helping the sun to shine brightly. But
some part of the log was always kept for the following
year not only to kindle a new Yule log but also to keep
away evil spirits.*

# CHRISTMAS TREE

*THE CUSTOM OF HAVING A DECORATED TREE AT CHRISTMAS originated in Germany and is associated with a legend about St. Boniface who, one Christmas Eve, cut down the pagans' sacred oak tree and instead offered them a young fir tree as a symbol of the Christian faith. Fir trees decorated with apples, sweets and paper roses were found in many German homes by the 16th century; just over a century later the custom was widespread in Germanic lands and candles and glittering decorations were added to the Christmas tree.*

*Prince Albert is credited with introducing the Christmas tree to Britain in 1841 but it had reached England a couple of decades earlier via German merchants and Court officials, and the custom was already popular in America because of German immigrants. But it was undoubtedly the Prince Consort's tree, brought from his native Germany and set up in Windsor Castle for his family, that captured public fancy. By the 1890s, one Covent Garden retailer supplied trees up to 40 feet (12.2 metres) tall and could boast of sales of over 30,000 a year.*

# CHRISTMAS CARDS

CHRISTMAS CARDS ARE A RELATIVELY RECENT INVENTION. THE first one was produced in 1846 by Sir Henry Cole, director of the Victoria and Albert Museum, England, and designed by a friend, John Horsely. It showed a cheerful family group raising their glasses in a toast and carried the inscription 'A Merry Christmas and a Happy New Year to You'. Sadly, the card was a commercial failure, selling less than 1,000 copies, but the idea slowly caught on and, by 1851, an English company was printing Christmas cards for the mass market. The real breakthrough occurred in 1870 when the halfpenny post was introduced for cards sent in unsealed envelopes; by 1880 the Post Office was issuing the familiar message 'Post early for Christmas.'

The first Christmas cards were often simply decorated calling cards, but soon sentimental snow scenes, angels, robins and nativity scenes appeared. By the end of the century the range of subject matter had expanded to include all the perennial favourites, many of them produced in three-dimensional or pop-up form. In 1893 a Royal Warrant was granted to the London designer and manufacturer of cards, Raphael Tuck.

19

# CHRISTMAS WREATHS
# AND RINGS

—◅≫—

*EVERGREENS HAVE BEEN USED SINCE EARLY TIMES TO MAKE
Christmas decorations such as garlands. The Victorians
introduced welcome wreaths, assemblies of holly, ivy, pine
cones and ribbons, which were hung on the front door to
welcome visitors. The tradition originated in
Scandinavia from whence it spread to Britain and
the United States.*

*Another ring of evergreens is the 'Kissing Bough'.
This is a half circle of evergreens with a ring of candles above
and red apples decorated with mistletoe below that is hung
from the middle of the ceiling like a crown. The candles are lit
and relit every day from Christmas Eve to Twelfth Night.
Lovers kiss under it and friends and families sing and dance
beneath it. The 'Advent Ring' is similar, except that it
contains no mistletoe and only four candles, one of which is lit
on each Sunday of Advent until by Christmas
all four are burning.*

# THE HOLLY
# AND THE IVY

*The holly and the ivy*
*When they are both full grown*
*Of all the trees that are in the wood*
*The holly bears the crown*

TRADITIONAL CHRISTMAS CAROL

*THE CUSTOM OF BEDECKING THE HOUSE WITH EVERGREENS DATES*
*back to pagan times when they were offered in homage to*
*woodland spirits and gods as symbols of everlasting life. Life-*
*giving qualities are particularly invested in the holly, with its*
*shining green leaves and striking red berries signifying male*
*sexuality. In combination with the female ivy, it promised new*
*life and fertility to the entire household. Conveniently*
*ignoring these ancient associations with fecundity,*
*the Church promoted holly as a symbol of good luck, linked*
*with Christ's agony and crucifixion: the sharp leaves*
*represented the crown of thorns and the red berries*
*His drops of blood.*

# CHRISTMAS CAROLS

*CAROLS DATE FROM THE 12TH CENTURY WHEN THEY WERE SIMPLY secular songs to be danced to on festive occasions. As it had done with other customs, the Church soon took over these jolly folk songs, imbuing them with religious significance by substituting the original texts with sacred or uplifting verses. They were not exclusively Christmas songs until the 16th century by which time ancient and new carols were being sung in almost every European language. This heyday of carols was shortlived; the Reformation and then Puritanism all but destroyed the carol tradition, except in Roman Catholic countries.*

*Carols were revived in the 19th century by folklorists devoted to collecting the fast-disappearing customs of 'Old England'. They were soon absorbed into the Victorian Christmas and became synonymous with Christmas hymns. Many new carols were written, often to traditional melodies. The custom of carol-singing by wandering musicians, usually collecting for charity, has ancient origins but dates mainly from the 19th century.*

# CHRISTMAS DRINKS

*THE TRADITION OF SERVING HOT SPICED DRINKS AT CHRISTMAS dates back to the Middle Ages when 'wassail' was drunk over the festive season, especially at New Year. Wassail comes from two Anglo-Saxon words meaning 'good health' and soon became identified with 'lambswool', a potent mixture of hot ale, roasted apples, sugar and spices. It was presented in a large wooden bowl, often decorated with ribbons and garlands, which was passed around from hand to hand in fellowship.*

*In some parts of England it was the custom for young men and maids to go from house to house with the wassail bowl, inviting the inhabitants to drink to the season and refill the bowl.*

*Apple-tree wassailing had a different meaning altogether. It usually took place on Twelfth Night in Devon and Somerset, where cider was drunk from the wassail bowl, then sprinkled on the apple trees to ensure fruitfulness during the coming year.*

# ƒANTA CLAUS

*THE FAMILIAR IMAGE OF SANTA CLAUS AS A PLUMP, WHITE-HAIRED old man complete with sled and reindeers is a 19th century American invention. Yet the legend of Father Christmas is both ancient and complex.*

*Two figures were combined to create Santa Claus. The first was St. Nicholas, a fourth century bishop who is patron saint of sailors, pawnbrokers and children. The second was the Christmas spirit, a mischievous, medieval figure who encouraged merrymaking, dancing and drunkenness.*

*By the 19th century, the Christmas spirit had taken on the characteristics of St. Nicholas, whom the Dutch settlers in North America called Santa Claus. According to the legend, the saint once threw some gold coins down a chimney which fell into a stocking that was hanging near the hearth to dry. This is the origin of the Christmas stocking. Santa's red robe is that of a bishop's, but his Arctic home, sled and reindeers come from Scandinavian Christmas myths. His traditional appearance, complete with fur-trimmed robe and sack of toys, was devised by Thomas Nast, whose drawing appeared in* Harper's Magazine *in 1868.*

# GIFT WRAPPING

SPECIAL CHRISTMAS WRAPPING PAPER AND DECORATIVE
*trimmings are relatively late developments, made possible
only in the 20th century by cheap colour printing. The
Victorians had to make do with brown paper, for that was all
there was, but in many ways this was an advantage; a
decorative wrapping, by necessity, had to be personally
created by the giver.*

*Many Victorians collected scraps, printed sheets of decorative
alphabets and pictures produced mostly in Germany, which
were stuck into special albums. At Christmas scraps were cut
out by the artistically inclined, glued in various designs on to
a package and then decorated with glittering spangles. A
handwritten message and a glossy ribbon completed the
effect. By the end of the century, pretty coloured borders and
cut-outs of angels and other Christmas motifs were being
produced, marking the beginning of commercialized
wrappings and decorations.*

*The custom of giving prettily wrapped gifts at Christmas was a German one introduced to Britain by Prince Albert who in 1841 gave presents to his own children on Christmas Eve, much to their happy wonderment. Before then gifts had traditionally been exchanged at New Year.*

# CHRISTMAS FARE

*EVEN IN THE HUMBLEST VICTORIAN HOUSEHOLD, CHRISTMAS dinner was the most lavish meal of the year. While the royal family in 1840 sat down to turtle soup, roast swan, beef, mutton, turkey, boar's head, mince pies and plum pudding, lesser subjects saved up for a large fat goose. This was the customary Christmas treat in the south of England while in the north beef was usually eaten; turkeys were rare until the 1870s.*

*Millions of poor households could only afford a Christmas goose by contributing throughout the year to 'goose clubs', usually run by public houses, and therefore condemned by moralists. Few families had the facilities for cooking it themselves so, on Christmas morning, long queues would form outside the local baker who charged a small fee for the use of his oven. The climax of the meal was a sumptuous plum pudding, after which mince pies might be handed around. These were once rectangular, representing the manger, and were often topped with a pastry baby; in Tudor times they were known as 'coffins' and contained minced meat.*

# CHRISTMAS PUDDING

*PLUM PUDDING, WHICH IS TRADITIONALLY SERVED AT CHRISTMAS,
dates back to the 18th century when sweet and savoury
puddings were common household fare. Ingredients included
spices, dried fruit, suet and meat. The puddings were not
specifically associated with Christmas and were called 'plum'
puddings as dried fruits were then known as plums.*

*Plum puddings were regarded as such a delicacy by foreigners
that George I, a German prince, wanted to eat plum pudding
at his first English Christmas in 1714.*

*From then on, a sweet plum pudding, without meat, was
served at Christmas in all but the poorest households. By
Victorian times, it was firmly enshrined in the Christmas
ritual, its preparation taking place on Stir-up Sunday, the
last Sunday before Advent. The pudding had to be stirred in
an anticlockwise direction by every member of the household.
Silver charms or coins were hidden in it by the cook, then the
pudding was wrapped in a cloth and boiled for at least seven
hours. It was always served with great ceremony at the end of
the Christmas feast, crowned with a sprig of holly and soaked
in flaming brandy.*

## GEORGE I's CHRISTMAS PUDDING

*1½lb shredded suet, 1lb eggs weighed in their shells,*
*1lb each dried plums, stoned and halved, mixed peel,*
*raisins, sultanas, currants, flour, sugar and breadcrumbs,*
*1 teaspoon mixed spice, 1 nutmeg grated, 2 teaspoons salt,*
*1 pint milk, juice of 1 lemon and*
*1 large wineglassful of brandy.*

# A CHRISTMAS CAROL

*DICKENS WAS INSPIRED TO WRITE* A CHRISTMAS CAROL *IN 1843 after visiting one of the Ragged Schools in the slums of London. These were institutions where dedicated teachers worked in appalling conditions to give poor children a basic education. Dickens was profoundly moved by the visit and was determined to write a pamphlet exposing the hardships of the poor when he hit on a better idea. He decided to write a Christmas story which would be read by thousands. The book, which was completed in six weeks and published at his own expense in time for Christmas, was a huge success and sold 6,000 copies on the first day of publication.*

A Christmas Carol *alerted the world to the terrible conditions of the Victorian poor and inspired many benevolent acts. As one factory owner in Vermont, USA, wrote: "I feel that after listening to Mr Dickens' a reading of* A Christmas Carol *I should break the custom we have hitherto observed of opening the works on Christmas Day."*

# CHRISTMAS CRACKERS

---

*CHRISTMAS CRACKERS ARE A LATE ADDITION TO THE CHRISTMAS festivities. They were invented in the second half of the 19th century by an enterprising young baker called Tom Smith who, while holidaying in France, noticed that bonbons were wrapped in coloured papers, prettily twisted at each end. He thought the idea would do well in England and set up a company to produce such wrappings. After a while, the sale of his novelty sweets began to decline, so he cannily incorporated a miniature explosive charge (a chemically treated card) so that children could have a tug-of-war over the confections. The 'crackers' were a huge success and soon Smith was enclosing tiny phials of perfume and miniature toys and games in his wrappers, adding a printed love message, motto or riddle as a novelty. By 1900 he was selling 13 million crackers worldwide each year, the majority of them at Christmas. Smith advertised his 'artistic crackers for table decoration' in colourful catalogues and it is interesting to note that many were more decorative and elaborate than the ones today.*

*In 1871 a Mrs Ewing noted the addition of the paper hat into crackers. "New-fashioned crackers", she observed, often contained a bonnet made of coloured tissue paper.*

# CHRISTMAS GAMES

*IN VICTORIAN TIMES, CHRISTMAS WAS A GREAT FAMILY OCCASION when both adults and children donned fancy dress, sang carols around the piano and played a variety of party games. One of the most ancient was Blindman's Bluff which dates from the Middle Ages, but other favourites included Hunt the Slipper, Forfeits and Musical Chairs.*

*One of the most exciting and dangerous games was Snapdragon, a traditional Christmas Eve game usually played by children. Raisins were placed in a large shallow bowl and brandy poured over the contents. As the lamps were dimmed and the candles extinguished, the brandy was set alight, and the assembled gathering quickly tried to snatch the raisins without burning their fingers, while one member of the family chanted the customary refrain: "Here he comes with flaming bowl, don't he mean to take his toll. Snip! Snap! Dragon. Take care you don't take too much. Be not greedy in your clutch."*

# BOXING DAY

*BOXING DAY TAKES ITS NAME FROM THE 'DOLE OF THE Christmas Box', a custom dating from the Middle Ages when alms boxes were placed in churches at Christmas to collect money for the poor. These were then opened on the day after Christmas and the contents distributed among the needy of the parish. Servants and apprentices also had their own personal 'boxes' – earthenware containers with a slit on the top – into which they put the tips and gifts they received during the year, especially in the days preceding Christmas; these were broken open on 'boxing' day when no further contributions were expected.*

*Although the Christmas dole came to an end with the Protestant Reformation, the custom of 'boxes' or gifts for farm labourers, apprentices, and servants continued. Throughout the 19th century and, until quite recently, 26 December was the day for giving money to the dustman, postman, paper boy and tradesmen who provided services during the year.*

# TWELFTH NIGHT

*TWELFTH NIGHT IS 6 JANUARY, THE DAY BEFORE THE Epiphany, the feast which celebrated the visit of the Three Kings to the Christ-child in Bethlehem. In Britain and America, it is now most notable as the day for taking down the Christmas cards and decorations. Once, however, it was the day for which a special cake was baked. In it was hidden a bean, a pea and some coins and whoever found the bean in his slice of cake became Lord of the Misrule for the evening. A mischievous figure, the Lord of the Misrule was in charge of the revels which, up to the 16th century, included masked balls and plays. Shakespeare's* Twelfth Night, *for instance, was written specially for such an occasion.*

*By the late 19th century in England and America, the Twelfth Night cake had become incorporated into the Christmas cake but in France the Galette des Rois is still eaten on 6 January. In Italy and Spain Twelfth Night is the traditional present-giving time for children and is a public holiday.*